TALL TALES

ALSO PUBLISHED BY 826MICHIGAN

- *If I Ever Saw Mr. JK, I Would Ask Him These Things*
- *Strange Mysteries*
- *Suddenly My Heart Stopped for Just a Small Portion of Time: Defining Moments*
- *This Pencil is My Most Important Possession*
- *Unsquared: Ann Arbor Writers Unleash Their Edgiest Stories & Poems*
- *Vacansopapurosophobia: Fear of a Blank Page*
- *Vacansopapurosophobia 2*

# TALL TALES

Involving whoppers, stretchers, lies (white & black), and wry observations on the human condition that are based, more or less, on real life events, but have, through a series of innovations & exaggerations, become ridiculously unbelievable (yet still somehow pertinent).

Published by BLOTCH BOOKS
*housed within 826michigan*
115 East Liberty Street Ann Arbor MI 48104
www.826michigan.org

Copyright © 826michigan and the authors
June 2008
All rights reserved

ISBN 0-9779289-5-0

All artwork created by Ian Huebert
www.themilkmachine.com
Book design by Amy Sumerton

# A BILLION AND ONE THANKS TO:

*All the folks at Childs Elementary for letting us infiltrate their classrooms: Jeff Petzak, Principal; Patricia Luckscheiter; Kylie Hill; Troy Hansbarger; Rochelle Sancho; Emily Hicks; and Rick Schaffner, Curriculum Director.*

*The Childs Parent and Teacher Team (PATT), as well as the parents who volunteered their time and energy, specifically: Lori Maranville and Michelle Wolf.*

*826michigan, especially: Erin Bennett, Thaddeus Blotch, Terry Carpenter, Chrissy Deiger, C. Jason DePasquale, Anne Ebbers, Mollie Edgar, Chandra Gill, Jennifer Guerra, Jen Halas, Jared Hawkley, Ryan Howard, Sean Murphy, Sydney Smith, Krysta Stone, Amy Sumerton, Amanda Uhle, and Chris Westoff.*

*Thanks, finally, to Ian Huebert for moving his pen about a page in such a way that resulted in our beautiful book cover and interior illustrations.*

# Tall Tales

| | | |
|---:|:---:|:---|
| Preface | xi | Jared Hawkley |
| Introduction | 1 | Thaddeus Blotch |
| Rally Ann Sally & McGladdin | 3 | Alex Maranville |
| My Cat, the Satellite | 5 | Riley Rawson |
| Bartholomew's Big Build | 7 | James Innes |
| Horse Miracle | 9 | Ashley Blackburn |
| The Evil Girl Behind the Mirror | 11 | Ashley Kurns |
| Dori Ann Yenderman | 15 | Elsie Joern |
| Fly-Wheel Green Ball | 18 | Renard Myles |
| The Story of Chicken Bob | 19 | Riley Mitchell |
| Tilly Tod | 22 | Sarah Vahosky |
| Bianca's Dream | 24 | Bianca Blackburn |
| Summer Vacation | 25 | Autumn Davis |
| The Brave Sewer | 27 | Betsy Bovich |

# Preface

OH! TO BE ten once again: that fleeting, elusive age that teeters between childhood and preteen-dom; the age when I had a knack for asking the big questions and for making up convoluted stories; the age when my imagination could still get the better of me; just exactly before the age when it became decidedly uncool to sit alone with a pen and knock words out like stones or dice.

Ten! when perfectly beveled ideas broke off of me like rubies and jewels, small, sharp, hard, smooth; wheelbarrows full of ideas, like a mother lode from the world's most bountiful mine wielding my pencil as my pickax. In those days I mined the ore of everything I saw, heard, or said; it was the age when I saw everything, right before the age I stopped seeing because things stopped being new.

Ten! that crude and shimmering age when I concerned myself mainly with pill-bugs and antlion pits, the best tree in the yard to climb, and how far I dared venture into the edge of town. How I made up what I didn't know. How I filled in the gaps of knowledge with imaginary bricks and a mortar made of humor (and yes! how this way of living mirrors the work of telling a tall tale).

Ten! when everything in the world was still coming together, still forming, just about to finally converge. How the world still appeared to be a bunch of incongruent parts, instead of one big system. How cause and effect, consequences—all the laws of life were erratic, even accidental.

Ten! when I knew innately that what I knew was transforming in small essential ways, and I couldn't quite grasp onto anything for sure—not yet—and that was why the world was so enthralling; when I could tie my shoes and be out the door in one single motion; when I thought I'd like to meet the man who could snake a twister and ride it through Tulsa and away into Death Valley.

All of the writers who invented the tales collected here are still caught in that strange and mysterious age. They understand the value of fiction, the virtue of a bendable truth. Theirs is the realm of the possible. Because of all of this, I half-expected the workshops to be a cakewalk.

At this point it is appropriate to note that I possibly had no hand in the actual conception of these stories; I feel lucky just to touch them in some way or another. What I did: during the first session of every workshop, I suggested they use themselves as main characters by exaggerating three of their talents or skills to ridiculous proportions. I also suggested they use an actual event from their lives as the conflict. After a few exercises and examples, I just set them loose. Having read most of the traditional American tall tales, I had a fairly definite expectation of how a tall tale should be, and of what the students would end up writing.

Somehow, in the mix of things, most of the students translated my "expectation" into just a "suggestion," and in a way, without my even knowing, it was the best translation a young writer could make in this context. That quality—substituting whim for a certainty—is the hallmark of an expert storyteller. I'm exceedingly pleased with how each and every writer's story turned out, because not one of them is anything like what I imagined.

No, these writers ain't Pecos Bills nor Sally Ann Thunder Ann Whirlwinds, and they surely ain't Babe the Blue Ox, neither. But they *are* keener than a city fox, and they know a truth that's truer than the dirt under your fingernails. Yes indeedy, they come from a place where truth means giving way to every little impulse, collecting the best parts of the normal and the regular and refurbishing them. What's a tall tale, after all, except the refurbished truth?

Above all, these young writers know, without anyone having to tell them, that a great story has got little to do with the facts; because the facts, friends, are only testimony. These here are Tall Tales.

— Jared Hawkley

*Introduction* | Thaddeus Blotch

WHEN I WAS your age, I didn't have it so easy. I know, I know: you think you've heard it all before, but if you'd just let me explain, you'd realize that you haven't.
As a young lad, you see, I wasn't such a grouch. The first thing that happened was, I was born with a rare heart condition that kept me bedridden for my first five years.

Perhaps you don't know what it feels like, having a heart like mine. Imagine that instead of a heart, you have a raisin. And not one of those plump California raisins, either. We're talking a raisin with cardiac arrhythmia, barely big enough to support my frail body—but I learned to live with it. I was generally a cheery chap in those days, and life was pretty okay.

Things only started looking glum when, moments before leaving me in a basket on the orphanage stoop, my mother told me that I'd never amount to anything more than an in-house editor for a non-profit writing organization. Coming from your own kin, that kind of talk hurts a little. For a few months, I just moped around the orphanage, oozing self-pity. One day, distressed by my mother's lack of faith in my abilities, I resolved to walk across the country and not stop until I crossed paths with my destiny.

Right away I jogged smack-dab into a thunderstorm. It was a mean ol' storm with mad winds that picked me up and ping-ponged me every which way, until finally I was encased in a giant raindrop that plummeted toward the barren prairies of Kansas.

Where it splashed, an enormous swamp sprang up, teeming with crocodiles and other fictional creatures living in a state of general discontent.

So there I was, stuck in the middle of this swamp, miserable as all-get-out because my boots were soaked, when I heard this feeble crying. Wading closer, I suddenly knew I had met my destiny, and it was shaped like a baby rhinoceros.

Unfortunately, my destiny was about to disappear in a quicksand pit. Acting quickly, I offered the poor fella a hollow log to grab hold of; to my surprise, he used it as a straw and drank up the grimy swamp-water until we found ourselves in a prairie once again.

Later, over a cup of tea, the very thirsty rhino offered to return the favor by granting me one wish. I wished for a good and healthy heart, so that I could do great and memorable things. And do you know what he told me? He said if I wanted to have a healthy heart, and not be so grumpy all the time, I should spend my life bringing joy and opportunity to young people.

What could I do but sigh mournfully? My breath wilted the flowers everywhere. Resigned, I trudged all the way to Ann Arbor, Michigan, and opened Blotch Books in the basement of an industrial park.

Well, friends, seventeen years and a move to downtown later, I'm still waiting to see if he was right. My heart is still soured and withered, and so many children running around all the time in their smelly diapers really exacerbates my sensory aversion, but I keep right on with publishing mediocre books with an incompetent staff, hoping for the day.

And I guess all of what I just told you would reasonably explain how I came to be the Blotch you know today, wouldn't it? But here's the thing: I MADE IT UP. All of it—every last lick. And the reason I did was because I have realized that LYING, OF ALL THINGS, BRINGS ME THE MOST JOY IN THE WORLD.

So, you're wondering, why am I such a crusty old miserly cynic? *Because that's the way I like it.* And also because I have a raisin for a heart. Deal with it.

*Thaddeus Blotch is owner, operator, editor-in-chief, the big cheese, grand pubah, AND grand master of Blotch Books.*

## Rally Ann Sally & McGladdin

### Alex Maranville

THERE ONCE LIVED a three-year-old boy who lived in the darkened woods. The boy's name was Rally Ann Sally and he loved heights. There were no skyscrapers in the area though, so Rally Ann Sally climbed trees. His favorite tree was a tree called McGladdin, which was 100,000 feet tall and touched the stars with its branches. Rally Ann Sally climbed McGladdin every day and also stood on the moon on the way up.

He lived in a small cabin with his only friends, Cat the Rat and Rat the Cat. Cat taught Rally Ann Sally to steal food from the bear's den. Rat taught Rally Ann Sally the most important skill of all: to climb trees! They also taught him how to get water by licking in the pond.

One day, Rally Ann Sally headed to the pond and was shocked to see that it looked like lungs in the summer heat. There was not a drop of water in sight. So Rally Ann Sally walked away.

The next day, Rally Ann Sally came with a shovel and dug fifty feet into the pond, but still could find no water. "Curses," yodeled Rally Ann Sally, and he walked away.

The day after that he came with a magnifying glass. He searched left and right for drops of water, but there was none to be found. "Oh, hilly billy!" cried Rally Ann Sally, and he walked away.

The next day, Rally Ann Sally came with his tongue because he had forgotten it at home the last three days. He licked everywhere but could find no moisture, so he walked away.

The whole experience left him speechless, and by the fifth day, Rally Ann Sally was sure this was a drought. Hints of a drought were all around, especially in the dead deer and other animals around. He knew he had to do something.

"Think, think," he said.

Suddenly, out of the corner of his eye, he saw McGladdin stretching high above him. He had an idea. It was probably the boldest idea Rally Ann Sally had ever had.

Rally started climbing McGladdin all the way to the clouds. Then, McGladdin started to shrivel and the gigantic tree started to fall. The huge trunk started to plummet toward the earth. Before Rally Ann Sally had time to think, he grabbed the clouds and climbed them to the top and started shaking them like crazy.

Rain started to fall. There was so much rain that all of the dead animals who had faded away of dehydration came back to life. Even McGladdin came back to life and its trunk towered over the forest again.

In the years since, many stories have been told about Rally Ann Sally and how he saved the forest from drought with the biggest rain shower that ever fell. Many say they've seen him waving from atop the clouds.

*My Cat, the Satellite* | Riley Rawson

THERE ONCE WAS a very rich cat named Weasley Billy Beasley Kitty Katty Smitty Smatty Crazy Cat "WEAZ" Rawson (don't ask me, he made it up himself). He came from a litter of forty-two kittens, each of whom had opposable thumbs and could talk, write, and read like people did. He spent a while living with his littermates, but after several years he decided to go out and seek his fortune.

Weasley found it, all right! He acquired so much gold, jewels, and gold dust off Ebay, the internet store, that his hoard stretched from Alaska to Florida. He, in fact, *bought* the land from Alaska to Florida so that he could store his treasure there. He also bought a huge castle that stretched across the whole of North America and hired servants to bring him dried gourmet fish flakes every day.

Weasley soon decided he would like some more stuff. Therefore, he went on Ebay (again) and bought a crown. The crown was very large, gold, and covered with real jewels. It had belonged to England's Queen Elizabeth; she had decided to sell it on Ebay and donate the money to her favorite charity (Garden Gnome Statue Rescue Home). He then went to a yard sale and found a coat made from the fur of purple lemmings that was covered in gold dust. That coat really sparkled! Weasley liked sparkly things. He had a veterinarian (who was also very rich) declaw him and replace his claws with gold and silver ones; 24K gold in front, sterling silver in back. It wasn't long after this that he got fatter and lazier and lazier and fatter than ever before (this was because he ate so many gourmet fish flakes).

One day, Weasley got so big from eating fish flakes that he was mistaken (and used) as a balloon entry in the Macy's Thanksgiving Day Parade! He got so mad, he bit through the ropes and floated up to space, where he became the largest and roundest satellite to orbit Earth.

It wasn't long before aliens from Pluto landed on him. They thought he was a planet, so they planted their flag and called him Planet Steve. By this time, Planet Steve had a curious ability to attract gourmet fish flakes. So suddenly, all the fish flakes in the universe flew toward Planet Steve and hit Weasley in the face. He licked his face and ate them all. Then he saw the aliens and thought they were also gourmet fish flakes. He tried to eat them as well, but they escaped in their spaceship and took off into space, where they flew to Earth and became the mystery that is known as "the crazy bathrobed cat lady that lives down the street."

*Bartholomew's Big Build*

James Innes

Once upon a time a long while ago there was a person named Bartholomew who could build as fast as lightning.

Rumor came around to the king. The king couldn't believe it, so he ordered Bartholomew to his castle and said to him, "Well, if you can build so fast, I want you to build me a building taller than my castle."

Now, this would be easy if the king was a normal king with a normal castle, but this king had the tallest castle in the world! On top of that, Bartholomew had none of the materials to build a building that big.

Just then, a thought came to him. Bartholomew's friend Noah had all the materials he needed! So, Bartholomew raced off to his friend's shop and asked him. Noah had all the materials he needed except for one screw! They were shocked!

Noah always had all the materials and now, half of the day had already gone by! They had to think quickly. They put the materials into a huge bag and brought along an empty bag. They each carried one sack. When they arrived back at the new castle location, they found the screw and dragged the bags back.

Since it was almost midnight, Bartholomew started taking the materials out of the bag, then building it, then putting it in the empty sack. When they finally got back to the castle, Bartholomew put the last screw in and saw that this castle was bigger than the king's castle.

At 11:58PM, he hurried the king outside to see it. The king could not believe his eyes! He compared it to his own castle and it *was* taller! The king looked at his watch and sure enough, it was 11:59PM. The king was so tired from staying up to see if Bartholomew would be able to make it, that he dropped right on the floor and fell asleep.

When the king woke up at 10:00AM, he found out that what he saw the night before really had happened. He gave Bartholomew a party and they had lots of fun. The king even made Bartholomew and Noah second hand thrones. After everything had settled and everything was calm, the king asked Bartholomew what he wanted to name his castle.

Bartholomew thought about this for a minute and then said, "The Empire State Building."

The Empire State Building stayed up for a long time after the king and Bartholomew were gone. In fact, it is still here today in New York, New York. The next time you visit there, I'm sure you'll think of it more than just a building.

# Horse Miracle

Ashley Blackburn

ONCE THERE WAS a girl named Nikki. She loved horses. She had three older brothers. One day Nikki's brothers went on a camping trip with their dad so it was only she and her mom.

A few days later her mom had a surprise for her. They were going to go horseback riding. Nikki's mom said she would like it because she did it when she was younger. So that day Nikki and her mom came to a farm. They said they were coming to go horseback riding, but it was closed so they had to wait another week. That week at school, she looked up all about horses and how to ride. Soon she knew everything about horses and how to horseback ride. Nikki's mom was really impressed.

Soon it came. Today was the day Nikki and her mom were going horseback riding. When they got to the farm there were a couple of people there, but it was mostly adults. When Nikki saw the horses she was going to ride, she froze. They were so beautiful.

"Nikki," her mom said.

"Wow, what just happened?"

"I don't know," said her mom, "but come on and let's go get your stuff on." So Nikki got her stuff on and got on her horse and rode. Soon it was time to go home.

The next day Nikki read the newspaper and on the front page it said: *Horse From Horseback Riding Farm is Missing.* She looked at the picture and realized it was her horse, Butterscotch! So she asked her mom if they could go back to the farm. But her mom said no. So later that night, Nikki sneaked out of the house and rode her bike to the farm. There was Butterscotch, sleeping on the grass.

"Nikki," said the horse.

"What the heck? Did you just talk to me?"

"Yeah, I did. All horses can talk!"

"Weird," said Nikki. "Why did you run away, Butterscotch?"

"Because I wanted to go home."

"Go home?" said Nikki.

"Yeah," said the horse. "I want to go back to the grassland where all my friends are."

"Well, I'll talk to the mayor."

So the next day Nikki sent a letter to the mayor telling him how Butterscotch wanted to go home.

A few months later, the mayor got the letter and told the farm to let Butterscotch go home. So now Nikki felt good and brave.

# The Evil Girl Behind the Mirror
## Ashley Kurns

YOU MIGHT HAVE heard those stories about cool inventors who invented the mirror. You may think that they used cool materials to invent it. Well, I'm here to say from experience, think again!

There is a cold-hearted, magic princess behind the mirror. She looks like everyone and everything. No, she's not Bloody Mary, but she's pretty close. Those two are sisters.

Now, they weren't always evil. In fact, they were beautiful princesses. They lived in a whole other world called Mirrotopia. It was a land like no other. But one day, an evil king took over the castle, and bewitched the two sisters' eternity! Now, nobody knew about these stories. These true, horrible stories. Until one day, this snoopy little girl named Paris made a horrible little wish . . .

"Let me get my toothbrush, Donnie!" Paris yelled, banging on the door, waiting for her stepsister Donnie (Donna-Marie) to get out of the bathroom.

"Go to Lilly and Dad's bathroom. Their toothbrushes are perfectly fine!" Donnie hollered sarcastically.

Donnie was a prep. A big prep. Paris was a nerd. A big nerd. And her parents, they were preps too. Big preps. This made Paris feel left out. But, sure enough, Donnie was the princess of the house. Not Paris.

"I wish I didn't have a sister!!" Paris yelled from behind

the bathroom door. All of a sudden, Paris heard a yelp. It was coming from the bathroom. Paris quickly ran in to see her sister gone and out of sight. Paris checked in the bathtub. No Donnie. She checked in the closet. No Donnie. She even checked in the toilet. Still no Donnie.

"What have I done?!" Paris cried while dropping to the floor. Out of nowhere, Paris noticed the window wide open. Paris got off the floor and closed the window.

"Ha, ha, ha, ha, ha!!" a voice screamed suddenly.

"Who, who's there?" Paris asked in a breathless tone.

"Oh, it's only the evil Bloody Macy. The sister of Bloody Mary. Your wish is granted. You don't have a sister anymore!" the voice hollered again.

"Come out, you freak! And give me my sister!" Paris cried.

"Turn around, you foolish girl! I'm in the mirror!" the voice hollered once again. Paris turned around, and to her surprise, there was a talking, evil witch in the mirror. She had a pale face, green rotten teeth, and a pitiful and utterly yuck face!

"Why, why are you doing this? Give me my sister, please!" Paris sobbed.

"Someone's coming! You keep quiet, you adolescent filthy child!" All of a sudden, Bloody Macy's face went back inside of the mirror.

"Honey bear, what is going on? I heard screaming and crying," Mom said with her petunia-red robe on, its ties dangling by their kitten, Jacks (they named him that because he jumps like jacks).

"Well, I um . . . I lost Donnie, sorta, kinda," Paris said with a fake and playful grin. Mom could see that Paris was hiding something. Paris looked through the mirror and Paris saw she and her mom standing inside of the mirror. She could have sworn she saw herself wink at her.

"Honey, where is Donnie?" Mom asked.

"Well, she went into the . . . " Paris felt something or someone thrash through her.

"She went into where, Paris?" Mom asked again.

"Into the kitchen," she lied. Mom sped down the stairs faster than you could say "see ya!" Then, Paris felt the object move out of her and move into the mirror. Paris quickly locked the door and moved closer to the mirror.

"Are you alone?" the voice shouted.

"Yes, yes I am," Paris answered, stuttering. The face appeared in the mirror.

"You dumb little spectacle!" Bloody Macy hollered. "You almost told that freaky mother of yours about the other world! You! Step in here! Now!" Bloody Macy hollered with her teeth crunching and her face turning bright red.

"But, but, but I, um. Please, no!" Paris sobbed.

"Now!" she yelled. Paris couldn't help but jump in!

"Paris, she's not in the kitchen! You're in big trouble!" Mom called from downstairs. That wasn't a good sign. Paris quickly jumped in the mirror. When Paris got in, it was pitch black. Then a dark blue light shined bright in her eyes.

"I will kill you! I will kill you and your stupid sister too! She sure has some mouth on that little body!" Bloody Macy hollered.

"No! Please, no!" Paris yelped.

"Leave her! We need her identification!" a voice hollered from out of the blue (or should I say out of the black).

"Thank you, missus," Paris thanked with a sniffle.

"Shut up, you little crybaby!" the voice hollered again. Paris looked for the woman, but then wished she hadn't. This woman was worse than Bloody Macy. In fact, compared to this woman, Bloody Macy would be an angel! This was Bloody Mary.

"Sorry, Mrs. Mary. I talk too much. I just want my sister back," Paris yelped even more. All of a sudden, Paris felt a pull on her arm. Bloody Mary was pulling her somewhere.

"Make sure you kill her on the way!" Bloody Macy yelled behind us.

"What's going on? I'm sorry, please!" Paris cried. Just then Paris felt power in her. She reached out and slapped Bloody Mary, stumbled her to the ground, reached in her pocket, and found a ray gun. She blasted Bloody Mary and Macy with the ray gun. At that very moment, everything started getting brighter and prettier.

"Why, thank you! Thank you so much, little girl!" Bloody Mary and Macy said, hugging her.

"You broke the spell, little girl!" Bloody Macy hugged even more.

"You're welcome, Bloody . . . I mean princesses," Paris said, hugging back. Then they stopped hugging and trotted off together.

"Paris!" she heard a voice yell.

"Hey, I recognize that voice!" Paris said, turning around to see Donnie. "I missed you sooo much!" Paris hugged her.

"You went through that much trouble for me?" Donnie asked.

"You bet, sis!" Donnie hugged back. Pretty soon the girls returned back home, with a hug and a kiss from Mom, and they lived happily ever after.

# Dori Ann Yenderman
## Elsie Joern

DORI ANN YENDERMAN was always the best at everything. When she was a little girl she could yell the loudest, spell the fastest, jump the highest, and eat the most out of all of nineteen older brothers. Everyone was jealous of her. All of the girls at her school in Mount Pleasant, Michigan were always mean. But she didn't care because her mom told her to always stand for yourself. Dori knew she could be the best at everything.

One day, a new girl came to her school. Katie Sue was a mean, nasty snob! Dori didn't like her at first sight. Katie was a total fake. She acted like a sweet girl in front of the grown-ups, but when she saw Dori, she had a huge glare. Dori thought Katie didn't like her because she was the best (until she met Dori).

"Dori Ann Yenderman, you're the most ugliest, dumbest, stupidest person I've ever met!" Katie said with a big frown on her face. "Well," said Dori, "at least I'm not conceited, a snob, and a fake, like you!" Everyone on the playground was gathered around like the planet was dying.

"That is . . . is . . . " Katie didn't have anymore words to say. She looked like she was thinking about what she would say next. Just before Dori was about to leave, Katie said, "Dori Ann Yenderman, I challenge you to a Mountain Test!" Everyone gasped when she said that. A Mountain Test is the hardest challenge in Mount Pleasant. It's an event that only men do. There are only three events, but hard events.

So that weekend Dori and Katie had the test. Whoever won got to be the best kid in the village, but the loser had to leave the state and never come back.

"Okay," said one of Dori's brothers. "The first event is to lift Bo and Mo." Bo and Mo were one-hundred-pound cows that live in the Dairy Field. "The person that holds them longest wins the first event!" Everyone cheered as Dori and Katie each got ready to lift a cow. "On your mark, get set, go!"

The two girls lifted their cows over their heads. Dori was really confident about the cows. Katie had gotten really weak from working herself all week. After twenty minutes Katie had dropped her cow on its back, and she lay down on the grass. Dori put her cow down carefully and ran to the other cow.

"You could kill a cow if it's on its back!" said Dori.

"Dori won the first event!" Everyone cheered for her. "Now, the second event: you have to sail your boat to the end of Gongongo Lake!" Gongongo Lake was the deepest little lake in their town. "All right, ready, go!"

Dori and Katie raced off. Dori's boat was old and little, and it also had some holes on the side. It was her grandfather's boat in World War II. Katie, on the other hand, had a big ship that looked like tar wood.

"Katie!" Dori yelled. "There are biting fish! They're attracted to tar and butter!" Dori was nervous.

"Dori Ann Yenderman, you're just trying to scare my wits!" Katie wasn't worried. She knew Dori was trying to scare her. But just before the finish line, Katie started sinking. Biting fish and crocodiles were chewing up her boat. "Help! Help! Man overboard! Where's my life raft!" Katie was yelling and screaming her head off. When she got to shore, everyone was cheering. Dori had gotten to the finish line before her.

"Oh, Dori Ann Yenderman, I will beat you!" Katie said, stomping and kicking mud.

"Okay, in the last event, you have to race across the U.S. You have a map with check points. Whoever gets back to the finish line first wins!" Everyone was cheering for them as they got ready. "On your mark, get set, go!"

The first check point was in St. Louis, Missouri. The next one was in Sacramento. Then they traveled to Austin, Texas where they stopped for coffee. Dori was in the lead, heading to

Louisiana. But Katie had so much coffee that she zoomed for Illinois. Dori was getting bummed. So she used all her power and made it to Mount Pleasant.

"Dori won!"

So, Katie had to move to Alaska. She was never heard from again. But Dori was now the bestest girl in Mount Pleasant!

# Fly-Wheel Green Ball
## Renard Myles

ONE DAY, MY brother Mikey and I were playing with a green ball. I threw it, but Mikey missed and the ball sailed like a fly-wheel.

It went through the kitchen, jumping on and off things. First, it jumped on a cup and Mom's purse. Then it jumped on two cartons of milk, a cup, and the hot chocolate container. Lastly, it landed in the cookie jar.

It was really awesome and cool until Mom yelled for us to stop playing with the ball in the house.

# The Story of Chicken Bob

## Riley Mitchell

ONE DAY IN a farmhouse, a chicken was born. He was scrawny like a stick. His mother said, "Oh my! What a tiny little . . . thing!"

His father said, "We'll never make a good, strong chicken out of him!"

So they tossed the poor chick out into the forest. In a few minutes, a wolf found him. This wolf (named Joe) was the strongest of the pack. He was also a very kind wolf, so he took the little chick to his house, and named him Bob. He groomed his feathers, and slept with him, and played hide-and-seek with him. The years went by fast. Soon it was Bob's fourteenth birthday. It was also the week of the Forest Olympics.

On the other side of the woods, the farm animals were preparing for the Forest Olympics. The schools took a holiday so that the kids could get in shape for the events. In the pigpen, the pigs lifted weights. In the chicken coop, the chickens did push-ups, and the cows were referees. There were Frisbees flying and trampolines here and there.

"Let's WIN! WIN! WIN! WIN! Go FARM ANIMALS!"

The Horse Choir sang the Fighting Farm Animal's theme song:

*Yes! YES! YES! We are the best!*

*Better than the rest! Go! FIGHT!*
*We can win! Stick up your feathers!*
*Brave through bad weather! Forever!*
*Together! Never break apart! Yea, these*
*Animals got fighting hearts! Go! Go! GO AND WIN!*

The wolves' side of the forest was chaotic, too! Everyone, including Chicken Bob, was toughening up for the Olympics. They were especially determined to win because it would take place in their forest. Joe was teaching Bob how to lift weights and run laps. But Bob was struggling.

"I . . . (*huff-huff*) . . . just . . . can't!" he panted.

"Aw, nonsense, Bob! You can! You just have to try!" Joe encouraged. Chicken Bob was tired. He was hungry. And he was SICK of lifting weights!

"I QUIT!" he yelled, running off into the Darker Side of the Woods.

"Bob! Wait!" Joe cried.

Bob had made it to the Fairy Tree. Lots of fairies were there, buzzing around.

"What's the matter, Bob?" the chief fairy asked.

"Oh, I'm training for the Olympics but it's so hard! I'm terrible at it! I can't do it!"

"You know, Bob . . . you can do anything you want to do, if you do your best," the chief fairy said. Bob smiled.

"Yeah! I guess I could!" He ran off.

Joe was running all over the forest looking for Bob.

"BOB! Come on out, Bob!" All of a sudden, he crashed into something. He looked up, dazed. "BOB! It's you!" he smiled. Then Bob and Joe walked home together.

That night, while Joe slept, Bob sneaked outside. He took a deep breath and . . . ZOOM! He ran as fast as he could all around the forest. Then he lifted twenty-five pounds in each claw. Finally, he did two hundred push-ups! Then Bob went to bed for a good night's sleep before the Olympics.

The next day dawned sunny and hot. The Farm Animals had a secret weapon. It was a giant creature named Mac, but everyone called him Big Mac. Big Mac was ready to fight. Then, from the forest, came a trumpet. Then, the singing!

*In any weather we will fight!*
*We are full of lots of might!*
*If you challenge us, prepare to lose!*
*But we aren't picky and we don't get to choose!*
*And we come out of the forest, heads held high!*
*O victory, victory is NIGH!*

The Farm Animals ran into the forest, with Big Mac behind them. The Olympics began. It was grueling battle. In five sweltering hours, they were tied! There were two events left! Up first was the trampoline. It was Bob's friend, Slippery the Snake, versus Jed the Pig. Jed was tough . . . real tough. Slippery wasn't as tough. Bob bit his nails all the way through the competition! In the end, Slippery won by two points. The two sides were tied. The last event was running. It was going to be Bob versus Big Mac. Bob gulped.

Bob put on his sweatband and took a deep breath. Big Mac cracked his knuckles. "Three . . . two . . . one . . . GO!" The referee yelled. Bob took off. Some say that he was as fast as a rocket. Big Mac and Bob were neck-and-neck through almost the whole race. At the very end, Bob slowed down a little. *You can do anything if you try! Go for it!* he thought. Bob thought of Joe, and the whole forest counting on him, and . . . he blasted across the finish line.

The forest erupted in whoops and cheers! A mob picked Bob up and carried him to the winner's podium. The chief fairy gave him a shiny gold medal. Then Bob ran to find Joe. Joe patted him on the back and whooped and cheered.

"I knew you could do it, Bob," he said. And Bob knew that he could, too.

### Epilogue

Bob became a legend in the forest. His parents visited him sometimes, and they always brought him presents. Years later, Bob got a family of his own, and he always told them this: "If you try your best, you can do anything you want!" And he knew that this was true.

# Tilly Tod
## Sarah Vahosky

ONCE UPON A time there was a boy named Tilly Tod. Tilly Tod was a very nice boy. He lived in a log cabin with his mother. He helped her every day. He would do the hard work that required his muscles and his mother did everything else. Every day his mother would tell him, "Be strong and confident and everything will be okay."

She also taught him that if he believed in something strong enough, he could change reality. Life was fine for a while. Everyday much like the next. UNTIL one day a witch came to visit. She was a Swedish witch, which meant she was a witch from Sweden. She was on vacation in America and happened to fly by Tilly Tod's house. Sadly, Tilly Tod did some mysterious thing to make her mad.

He began to talk to the witch about her vacation. You see Tilly Tod was very friendly. Unfortunately he happened to mention that he thought Sweden was a cold and ugly place. He then said, "I'll bet you like it here much more."

The witch became very mad and said in a mean voice, "Tilly Tod, for opening your big mouth and insulting my country, you will turn into a monster at the age of thirty-four. You will be forced to live in a swamp."

Fortunately, Tilly Tod was a nice boy who was a bit psychic like his mom. Not as strong as she, since everybody knows it runs stronger in women. Sadly, Tilly Tod's little bit of psychicness did not help much, because he turned into a monster anyway and moved to live in the swamp near his mother's home.

"That is such a stupid story, Rosie!" teased John.
"Well, you really are a wimp," laughed Rosie.
"Okay, I'll go if you come with me," urged John.
They decided to go together. The walk to the swamp took a long time. They were tired when they arrived.
"Okay, so where is he?"
"He's here. You see, the witch had a funny way of doing things. She asked Tilly Tod what the worst possible monster might look like. Being a young boy who wants nothing to do with girls, he said, 'Please just don't turn me into a . . . '" said Rosie with a smile.

# Bianca's Dream

## Bianca Blackburn

Once upon a time there lived a girl named Bianca. She had a lot of problems. She had horse legs. Everybody teased her. But she ran so fast, she was the fastest runner in the world! And she was only in first grade!!!!

After school, she went home, and she told her mom she was tired and just wanted to go to bed. So she went to bed.

When she woke up, she was on a different planet. She walked around and saw a person that looked just like her. She realized that everybody looked the same! She lived there for two years. Every day they got meaner and meaner and meaner and meaner.

One day they were so mean, they teased her and made her cry and stole her stuff. For two years they just played games with their cool legs. But when she woke up one morning, the people-horses had turned evil! So she used her legs to run around the whole world trying to find home. She woke up to her mom saying, "Wake up, wake up, it's time for your first day of school!" She was dreaming the whole time!

# *Summer Vacation*
# Autumn Davis

IT WAS SUPPOSED to be a day of peace and quiet. Everybody was relaxing in the sun on summer vacation. While a bunny (Tanya) and a turtle (Elena) were watching television in their bathing suits, *ding* went the door.

"Elena, go get the door," said Tanya.

Well, the thing was, Elena wasn't the fastest walker in the world. She would take her time walking to the door.

"Elena, go get the door!" Tanya said again. "Oh, never mind." When Tanya went to the large, twelve-foot door, a little Girl Scout was knocking.

"Hello?" said Tanya.

"Hi, I'm a member of the Girl Scout Academy of the Fourth Grade Society Girls. Would you like to buy some cookies?"

"Oh, no thanks, but, uh, you can leave now please, bye-bye!"

"Tanya, is that a Girl Scout selling cookies?" said Elena.

"Dang, uh, no, no, that's just your imagination," replied Tanya.

"Hi, would you like some cookies, whoever you are?" asked the Girl Scout.

"Yeah, sure. Tanya, buy me some cookies," said Elena.

"No" said Tanya, very annoyed.

"Well, I thought you were going to say that," said the Girl

Scout. Suddenly—zip—the Girl Scout unzipped herself and appeared to be . . . Dr. Flamingo (just call him the Dr. for short).

"Dr., you knew that my sister would fall for the whole Girl Scout thing because she loves the cookies. You also knew I would say NO, didn't you?!" Tanya's eyes grew as big as the twelve-foot doorway with curiosity.

"Yes, I did," answered the Dr.

"Oh, would you keep quiet already?!" shouted Elena.

"Okay, I get that, so what now, are you going to tell me what your secret plan is?" asked Tanya.

"Yes I will after this! AH-HAHA HA!" *Swish!* Suddenly something came down right out of the clear blue sky. It was a lock to keep Tanya's arms and legs from moving.

"Okay, now I will tell you. I'm going to go to all the houses in the entire neighborhood dressed up like a Girl Scout selling cookies. Whether they say yes they want some, or they say no thank you, I'm going to press a button that's in my pocket and it will bring down the locks like you're in and lock them up. Later, all of them will have to wear a headband that is blue. The headband will control their every move. Then soon I'll control the whole neighborhood! MWA-HA ha ha! I don't need to worry about you now because you are all locked up," said the Dr.

"Oh really?" said Tanya.

*Whoop!*

"How did you get out of those locks?!!" cried the Dr.

"I got out with my sister's help."

"Yeah," said Elena, "I heard a commotion, and since you forgot to lock me up I was able to come see what was going on."

"Oh yeah, I think you're forgetting something else . . . oh, I don't know, maybe in your pocket," said Elena. Elena was holding up the Dr.'s remote.

"Oh no, not the little remote! I use that to unlock my special locks and control all the blue headbands. Please be careful with it. It's really special and dangerous!" cried the Dr.

"Well, it's in safe hands now," said Tanya.

"Your evil plan has been foiled!" said Elena.

# The Brave Sewer

## Betsy Bovich

Once upon an ugly time, there lived a kind, smart woman who was suddenly awoken by a bullet shooting through her man-made door. As she heard the boom, she jerked up suddenly. Her brown, long hair followed her head as it jerked. Her hazel eyes looked petrified.

It was the early 1860s and the war of the nation was on. Listie (the kind woman) rushed out of her tiny bed and threw on her navy blue dress in thirty seconds flat (that was slow for her). But before I get to "what happens next," let me tell you about how wars were basically out in her yard. She helped every soldier. She could heal a man no matter the problem.

Let's get back to the story: "Lady, I order you to leave the room!" the soldier said. Listie didn't respond.

"Don't make me ask again," he said.

Listie had figured out the man was a Union soldier coming to get her. (Listie was a Confederate.)

Listie had read a book called *How to Escape Union Soldiers for Dummies*. One of the chapters was "How to Jump Out a Window Without Dying."

*Perfect!* Listie thought.

"A rope and a comfy blanket," Listie quickly said.

She hopped out of the window safely.

She hopped onto her horse but as soon as she thought she was safe, the horse collapsed.

She looked at a hoof and it was bleeding like crazy, almost making a river. Of course, she could heal anything. But she realized this one would take a while so she left the horse.

Eventually, they caught brave Listie and took her to Alexandria, Virginia. That's the end of Listie's story.

INDEX

*aliens,* from Pluto, 6
*alternate worlds*
    Horse-leg world, 24
    Mirrotopia, 11
    Planet Steve, 6
*animals*
    horses, (see *horses*)
    kind wolves, pigs, and chickens, 19
    resurrection of dead, 4
*ball*
    jumping around the kitchen and landing in the cookie jar, 18
*bathroom*
    stories that contain no mention of, 3, 5, 7, 9, 15, 18, 19, 22, 24, 25, 27
    the hogging of, 11
*boat,* tar and butter, 16
*bullies*
    who act like fakes, 15
    who look exactly like you, 24
*clouds,* the shaking of to produce rain, 4
*coffee,* the beneficial effects of, 17
*contests,*
    Mountain Test, 15
    The Forest Olympics, 20
*cows*
    as referees, 19
    on their backs, 16
*different planets,* waking up on, 24
*doors*
    man-made, 27
    twelve-foot, 25
*drought,* 3
*fish*
    biting (tar and butter), 16
    dried gourmet flakes of, 5
*forest* (see *woods*)

*games*, playing with your cool legs, 24
*home country*, accidentally insulting, 22
*horses*
    collapsing, 27
    Horse Choir, 19
    horse legs (problematic), 24
    horseback riding, 9
    missing, 9
    talking and/or singing, 10, 19
*kid*, best in the village, 16
*life*, coming back to, 4
*mayor*, writing letters to, 10
*monster*, turning into ~ and moving into the swamp, 23
*moon*, stopping to stand on, 3
*ray-gun*, as a means to break a spell, 13
*running*
    as a means to winning, 17, 21
    faster than anybody else, 15, 24
*siblings*
    disappearing, 12
    evil (see *witches*)
*throwing a ball*, 18
*tongue*, the forgetting of at home, 4
*tree* (ind.; for collective trees, see *woods*)
    that touch the stars with its branches, 3
    The Fairy Tree, 20
*war*, basically in your backyard, 27
*witches*
    evil sisters, 13
    from Sweden, 22
*woods*
    darkened, 3
    Darker Side of the, 20

*true stories*

← TALL TALES

*rotabucnI*, 9
*sad face*
    trying and failing to make one, 29
    upon hearing bad news, 26
*science experiment*, broken glass from, 4
*snacks*
    peanut butter with apples, 3
    Superman ice-cream, 25
    trying to get them to safety, 13
*tears*
    alligator, 16
    crocodile, 26
*test*, of 136 questions, 21
*underwear*, going to bed in, 16
*water slide*, green, 30
*weird squirrel who lives in a hole*, 28
*yelling*
    not coming out right, 10
    over the ocean wind, 13
*you*, the most incredible machine, 8

*alien*, who just burped, 22
*babysitter*, who is enormous, tall, and fat, 24
*baseball*, playing right after getting one's cast off, 14
*bathing suit*, 12
*beard*, grown out of laziness, 3
*blossom*, that lands right on your head, 27
*cats*
> cat mansions and snake caves, 17
> whose eyes twinkle like the stars and dance like the moon, 5
> who knock over plants and get stuck in trees, 23

*contact lenses*, accidentally drinking, 16
*dogs*
> a four-legged yellow thing, 10
> with bloody paws, 4

*EXPLODE!*
> bursting open, 21
> the feeling that you are going to, 8

*fire*, inside Daddy's car, 26
*forehead*, red as the devil's face, 19
*gameboard*, making as a partner project, 29
*googly-eyes*, 10
*grandparents*, 3, 15, 17, 23
*hamsters*, with pink dots on the forehead, 17
*hiding places*
> inside cabinets where blocks are stored, 5
> under the deck, 4

*interview*, done over a bowl of Corn Flakes, 25
*looking like a whale without water*, 14
*lost*, black and grey kitten, 5
*machine*, that lives in a closet, 7
*peanuts that remind one of the ocean*, 19
*phone call*, bad news, 26
*rain*
> as the tears of a loved one, 3
> freezing rain and hail, 15
> like hammers hitting the floor, 19

# INDEX

## My Water Park Birthday Party | Marisa Fitch

IT WAS THE day before my birthday. My birthday party was at a new water park, so we got a room. It was awesome. The water park was very fun. They had a green slide. It was all dark . . .

I went to the room. I got to get my bed first. I was so happy I got the top, and my friend came and she got the other top because there were two beds. We were at the water park 'til nine-thirty.

In the morning IT WAS MY BIRTHDAY! Then we went to the water park again in the morning.

After that we got to go to the arcade. It was so fun. I was nine that day on October 20. It was so fun at the water park. Maybe I might have it there again next year. When I'm ten.

# *Partners*

## Autumn Davis

ONE DAY, EVERYBODY was sitting in their seats and . . . Rebecca, Jordan, Ashley, and I were talking, when our teacher told us that we were going to do a project with partners. The project was making a gameboard. Everybody jumped right up and picked their partners. Rebecca and I were about to be partners when Ashley and Jordan ran up in front of us and asked us both if we wanted to be their partners.

Rebecca and I were stunned. We told them that we were going to be partners, but they suddenly said that we're always partners. They tried to make a sad face, but they couldn't. Rebecca told them both that she'll be their partner next time.

About five minutes later, I asked them if they wanted to be partners. Jordan and Ashley just looked at each other and said, "Okay, sure." Later on, Rebecca and I felt kind of bad, so we walked up to Jordan and Ashley and asked if they were okay about the partners. When we asked them, they forgot about the whole thing. We were relieved to hear that. Everybody was okay with their partners and started on their game board again.

Mother's Day. Spring was sad though. I never got to see the tree very much because I was at school eight hours a day. When I did though I have to say, we had the most interesting chats. My friends used to think I was crazy, talking to a tree, but I think they're the ones who were crazy. The ash tree tells me a lot. It tells me about the birds in its branches and the weird squirrel that lives in a hole. The stories were quite interesting and every time the tree told me a story it was different from the other ones.

Winter was what season I dreaded most. I always would worry about the tree being blown over by monstrous winds. I was always inside on winter days so all I could do was sit, and watch the tree freeze. I often had nightmares about the tree being destroyed and never really paid attention to them until that frightful afternoon.

I was walking home from school one spring afternoon filled with joy. I skipped from the bus stop to my house. I threw aside my backpack and went trotting to my backyard. My jaw dropped when I saw what my dad was doing. I saw only four things at the moment. I saw an ax, a chain-saw, a stump, and the branches that used to be the ash tree. Suddenly everything was a blur. Tears spilled out of my eyes like crazy as I ran inside the house. I headed straight for my room and slammed the door.

After I cried for a few minutes my parents came in. They explained to me that a nasty beetle had gotten it and that it would have died anyway. After a few weeks, I got used to not having the tree around. I found other friends who had just as good of stories. Even though I have those friends too, I'll never forget the wonderful friendship.

# The Tree

## Alex Maranville

THE TREE WAS of great love to me. It gave me shelter and warmth when I needed it and seemed to always be there for me. "The grandest tree in the neighborhood!" my friend Warren once had said to me. I knew his words spoke true and so did he. The tree was an ash tree and every time I went outside I took a moment to adore it.

Fall was my favorite time because of the tree. It had beautiful leaves from red to yellow to orange to green. It provided shade when I raked the leaves and when I was bored I could always find the most interesting species of bugs on the trunk if I looked closely.

Summers were also quite fun. The ash tree provided shade on the hottest of days. It let me relax when I wanted to rest and let me run around it when I wanted to run. I often brought a soccer ball into the shade and started playing with it until I could play no longer. My favorite part about summer though was when I could hear the tree's leaves whispering to me. They didn't whisper in a normal voice though, and that is what made it so special. It whispered by shaking its branches and letting the birds sing and letting the wind howl and most importantly dropping the last blossom it had, and letting it land right on my head.

Spring however was nothing more than beauty when I saw the tree. It had hundreds of small leaves ready to sprout on it. I often picked the leaves of the ash and gave them to my mom for

## Part 2: The Fire

### Alexis McGhee

ONE DARK NIGHT, my mom and I were watching a movie. Suddenly, the phone rang: *Ring-ring.* I answered.

"Hi Daddy!" I said, excited.

Dad said, "I need to talk to Mommy," in a scared voice.

I got scared, so I gave Mom the phone. Three minutes later my mom yelled, "Go get your coat!" Now I was scared out of my mind! I started crying, and so did Mommy. We rushed to the car.

"Mommy, is Daddy okay?" I said with big crocodile tears coming down my cheeks.

Mommy said, "Daddy has had a fire in his car." At that moment I thought my dad was going to die.

Five minutes later, we saw Dad. He was on the side of the road. I ran to give him a huge hug.

I asked, "Are you okay?"

"I'm fine," he said. The fire in the car engine went out. We went home. We all had hot cocoa and we watched a movie.

*THE END*

After that I felt so relieved. I could tell my mom was, too.

big and tall and fat! Sally went to her room to read and do her homework. She tried to forget about Bertha but she couldn't. After she was done with her homework, she drew pictures. Eventually she forgot about Bertha. Her mom came home and Sally was sleeping.

When Sally woke up the next morning, Bertha was already there. Bertha was eating breakfast. Sally got some Corn Flakes and sat next to Bertha to have a conversation with her.

As they ate, Sally kind of did a little interview. First, Sally asked where she was from. Bertha said, "Russia." Then Sally asked if she had any sisters or brothers. Bertha said, "Two twin brothers."

Sally said, "Okay."

Next, Sally asked where she lived. Bertha said, "In Ann Arbor." Then came the final question. The question was if she had any kids or pets. Bertha said, "Two dogs, three parakeets, and one cat." Then Sally asked one more question: what were the pets' names? Bertha said that the dogs' names were Spunky and Tazzy, Taz for short. Next came the birds, and she said their names were Pumpkin, Cootie, and Chloe. Then came the cat's name, and her name was Stripes.

Bertha took Sally to school, and after school Bertha and Sally went to the mall. When they got home Sally told Bertha that was the most fun she ever had. Bertha smiled and gave her a hug. Sally realized that looks and size don't matter. Next, Sally said, "Can we hang out tomorrow?" Bertha said, "Sure." She also said they could go to the park, and maybe get some ice cream.

After school the next day, they went to the park. They got ice cream; Sally got Superman, and Bertha, butter pecan. They had so much fun talking and getting to know each other.

Sally did not realize how much fun Bertha is! Sally loves Bertha. After the outing, they went home to watch a movie.

Now Sally loves Bertha, and will always love her. Sally still realizes that looks and size don't matter, it's all about being nice to each other!

# Sally & the Gigantic Babysitter

## Taylor Hosein

O NCE THERE WAS a girl named Sally. She was in the fourth grade. Her parents always had to go to work. They didn't come home until ten-thirty at night, so she needed a babysitter. Her babysitter's name was Jamie.

Sally loved her babysitter so much! One day Jamie was getting married and moving to California. Sally did not believe her mom, so Sally went to Jamie's house to see if it was true or not. It turned out it was true. Sally was so mad and sad. She did not know what to do!

Sally was really confused. She was scared that her parents wouldn't find a new babysitter that she liked as much as Jamie, but they did in about two weeks. Sally wanted Jamie back so badly.

The next day the new babysitter was at Sally's house, and she had to meet her. Sally didn't want to go home. She was scared that she wouldn't like her new babysitter. She was thinking a lot of negative thoughts.

When Sally got home, she was shaking so bad, and she was afraid to go in the house. When she went inside she saw an enormous tall and fat babysitter. Sally was so scared. First, she asked for her name. Her name was Bertha. Sally had never heard that name before!

Sally thought that name was really weird! She was still really scared of Bertha, so scared she had no idea how Bertha got so

# The Special Cats

## Sydney Maranville

ONE TIME, WHILE the screen door was open, a cat named Cobbie got out and got killed by a coyote. Can you believe it?

My grandma and grandpa buried Cobbie in a special place surrounded by flowers. They marked the place with a stone. They were very sad, so they got new kittens named Sadie and Peppi. They were so cute!

I can tell you, they were very strange and weird cats, but they were still cute. They knocked over the plants while Grandma and Grandpa were gone. They climbed up a tree and couldn't get down.

When I visited, I played a lot with them. We played ball and hide-and-seek in the garden.

Sadie was rowdy and liked to get into trouble. Peppi just liked to be held. Sadie loved to go in the basement because she got hot and needed fresh air. What a smart kitty!

Sadie and Peppi are outside cats and are fast runners. I sometimes worry they could get hit by a car. They sometimes jump and pounce on people and that means they are playing.

If you went to the farm, the kittens would be so cute and that is why I'm telling you about them. I miss them now that I'm here in Michigan, but I'm lucky to have my own cat named Annie.

passed! Unfortunately, Morgan had not.

The next day at nine o' clock, I went to Mrs. Lucksheiter's room—a fourth grade room. I went there for math. When I came, everyone was staring at me like I was an alien who'd just burped. It was that bad!

But after a while, I started to fit in. Then everyone started asking why I was there. So I'd have to tell the whole story over again.

Finally, summer came. I was free of the math's wrath . . . 'til next year.

# Why Me?

## Kellie Beck

UGH . . . *MORNINGS*, I thought.

It was a cool October morning and my hair blew in the wind. I thought it would be like any other day . . . man, was I way off!

Earlier in the year I had told my teacher that the math our class was doing was way too easy. Well, today something happened. Mrs. Luendowski, our principal, said I was going to take a test to see if perhaps I could make it into a fourth grade math class, even though I was only in third grade!

Well, as you can guess, I was excited. I headed off to my class and told Morgan, my best friend, about it. I was so excited when she told me she was going to take it, too! I felt like I could burst open!

After school, I went home and told my mom. Of course, she was excited too.

A few days later, Morgan and I started the test. You know how many pages there were? Eighty-nine! And there were one hundred thirty-six questions! It took me practically the whole day. By the time we were done, it was already recess time. Morgan and I ran out and started singing, "Celebrate good times, come on!"

Soon it was time to go home.

One day, while I was going costume shopping for Halloween with my mom, her cell phone rang. It was the principal, and I'd had a black one, and my sister and I had blue ones.

After it stopped storming, the Tigers took the field again and we sat in someone else's seats with our coats on. The final score was Tigers 12, Royals 9. We won! I was so happy and so was my dad. That was the best baseball game I ever went to.

# The Baseball Game

## Ashley Blackburn

ONE DAY I was on my way to Tiger Stadium with my family. They were playing against the Royals. When we got to the stadium we got some drinks and some hot dogs before we got to our seats.

When we got to our seats the game was about to begin. At the third inning, it was half time. We were still sitting in our seats, and I heard a man call: "Peanuts! Get your fresh peanuts here!" As I got to the peanut man, I gave him the money for two peanut bags.

We went back to our seats and I spilled peanuts *everywhere*. I remember stepping on the peanuts and hearing them *crunch,* and then I looked down and saw crushed peanuts everywhere. They reminded me of the ocean.

I wanted to keep crushing peanuts, but my dad said, "No." So I started crushing them on my forehead which felt like hail hitting me in the face, but I got used to the feeling and started to like it. Soon my forehead was as red as the devil's face. I stopped and tried to find something else to do.

In the sixth inning, big thunderclouds came and it started to sprinkle. We had to take cover.

By the time we got to the stadium it started raining so hard that it was like hammers hitting the floor. They covered the field with a tarp that looked like the American flag. My dad bought us all raincoats to keep us dry. My dad had a yellow one, my mom

"I want that one," I decided.

"Okay, how about we get that one and this one." My grandma pointed to a cute brown and white one.

"Okay," I said. We told a store employee.

He said, "What cage would you like?"

"We totally forgot about that," said my mother. After five minutes they decided on a glass cage about three-by-one.

"Okay," said the store employee. He put the hamsters in a box and we left.

# Pet Store

## Jake Clark

"ARE WE ALMOST there!!?" I screamed.

"Calm down, Jake," said my unexcited grandmother.

"The pet store is near," input my mother. My mother, grandmother, and I were going to the pet store, where my grandmother would get two pet hamsters. Our car rounded a turn and I saw Petco!

"Oh yeah, oh yeah!"

"If you're like this in the store, the manager will kick us out," my grandmother said.

"Ohh fine," I said, disappointed.

As I walked into the store, I questioned, "Where are the hamsters?" Apparently no one heard me because there was no reply.

I looked around. "Ohh," I gasped. The store was huge, from cat mansions to snake caves.

"There's the hamsters!" I told my mom.

"Okay," she replied back. When we got to the right aisle, I saw so many hamsters that I literally almost fainted!

"Wow, that's a lot of hamsters," I declared.

There were hamsters from white with black spots to brown with a pink dot on the forehead. I decided I wanted one with all grey hair and red eyes. It was the only one up and running around.

there was one couch, one chair, a bed, a sink, and one bathroom. There was no TV. While my sister and my brother explored the room, my mom and I remembered that we had no toothbrushes or pajamas or fresh clothes to wear. So we all went to bed in our underwear. My mom and I went to bed in the big bed and my sister and brother slept on the floor. We were still waiting for grandma's plane.

I realized I had left my special Pooh Bear at home. I could not remember a night I had slept without him. I cried myself to sleep.

The next morning I got up and went to the sink. I wanted to get a drink of water. I saw my grandma on the chair.

*She must have come in a taxi*, I thought in my head. "Hi," I said. She waved at me.

I saw a little glass of water and I was very thirsty so I drank the entire thing. Then I read the phone book until my mom got out of the shower.

"Hey Grandma," she called, "don't let anyone drink that glass of water by the sink because it has my contact lens in it."

I froze. "I drank it," I said in a cracking voice.

My mom took one look at me and started to laugh harder and harder. I burst into tears . . . big alligator tears. My mom stopped and looked at me. I said I was sorry. She said it was okay.

We drove home . . . my mom looking out of one good eye.

# One-Eye Disaster
## Hannah Wolf

WE WERE GOING to the airport to pick up my grandmother and it was raining. A few minutes later it turned into ice . . . slow, slow, slow, and slower . . . then it stopped. A little while later it started up again and went so fast I could barely see. We pulled into the airport and my mom got out and went into the airport with my sister and the baby-bag. My brother and I got out too. We waddled over the thick ice to get to the airport doors.

When we got inside the airport, the whole place was empty. My brother and I looked around and my mom went to go change my sister and give her a bottle. When my mom came out of the bathroom, she put my sister down and the baby zoomed across the floor.

My mom looked over at the electric sign and had a look of disappointment on her face.

She said in a dry whisper, "All the flights are canceled or delayed." With sadness in our hearts we skittered to the car. We realized the thick ice on the road was too slippery . . . we would never make it home without getting in a crash.

An officer in an orange vest stood at the exit of the airport. He waved his hands, motioning us to a big building. We looked up and saw: HOTEL.

We got the last room. It was a gross hotel even though the lobby looked nice. In our room the cups were all dirty and

# Broken Leg

## Seth Schubert

ONE DAY I was climbing a tree with my friend Ty. I climbed to the very top. I felt my leg slip. I thought to myself, *I'm going to fall!*

On the way down my leg hit the ground and a tree branch. I felt like I died! My leg hurt so bad. My friend said that I looked like a whale without water. Ty went to get my mom. I was knocked out cold. Ty said I hit the ground hard. When I got to the hospital I woke up but they put me right back to sleep for surgery.

When I went to school the next day everyone felt bad for me. I told them I was okay.

Two weeks later I got my cast off and played baseball right after that.

over the ocean wind, "C'mon, Chathu! Come deeper!" which I did, until I couldn't pull my pant legs up any higher.

"Can I get my pants wet now?" I called to my mom, who was sitting on the shore.

"Yeah, sure, if you want to," she replied.

I was glad to at least get her permission, but I still wasn't sure if I liked the idea all that much. I carefully waded in more, and more, and more, but I still somehow managed to stay dry, that was, until . . . *whoops!* . . . I slipped and lost my footing, then *splash!* I landed smack on my behind and sat on the sandy bottom of the ocean.

The freezing water hit me like needles, and the rigidness ran once more through my body. It pinned my arms to my body.

The cackling sound of laughter from Susiru and Kaveesha filled my ears, and my mother's teasing taunts rang over to me: "Is that wet enough for you?"

I shakily stood up and shook my arms dry the best that I could. There really wasn't any point in doing so, as I was soon going to find out, because right after I did that, *whoosh!* A giant wave swept under Kaveesha, Susiru, and I, and carried us toward the shore, practically throwing us on top of our mothers, who were trying to get the snacks to safety. Unfortunately, they were too slow, and the wave picked up the snacks (but thankfully not our moms), and took them out into the ocean.

The three of us older kids scrambled out into the water and grabbed the snacks, which were fortunately dry in the plastic beach bag. *What a way to spend a day at the beach,* I thought exasperatingly, as I plopped down to eat some Pringles.

# *Splash-Out!*
## Chathu Jayatissa

"**W**E'RE HERE!"

"Finally!" We all tumbled out of my uncle's crowded car. We were at the beach in Galle, Sri Lanka, the city I was born in and that the rest of the family grew up in.

I was there with my oldest uncle, my aunt, my mom, and three out of my seven cousins: Kaveesha, the oldest of the three (who's two years younger than me), Susiru, the middle kid of the three (who's in preschool), and Sithila, the baby (who's not yet in school). This was going to be an interesting day at the beach, I could tell . . .

I was the only one who didn't have a bathing suit on, but I didn't care. I was happy enough just to be there, and I would be careful not to get my clothes wet. Kaveesha and I were in the lead, running ahead to find a spot to leave our things while the others ambled on behind us. We soon found a place to leave our stuff, and Kaveesha immediately kicked off her flip-flops and threw off her clothes. She ran to the water in her swimsuit, while I also kicked off my Crocs and followed Kaveesha to the water more slowly. I didn't want to get my clothes wet, just as my mother had told me not to do. A rigid coldness ran through my body as I dipped my foot into the freezing water. I carefully waded in deeper, pulling my pant legs up higher with each step.

Meanwhile, I was trying to ignore Kaveesha, who was yelling

That show was kinda nice. I guess I will be safe here. I'm snuggled up and cozy . . . *Aahhhh.* I am going to live! (Maybe just not on Mars.)

but I don't know what this is. What if it's some . . . some
. . . what do you call it? A *brain eating* machine! Help! Help!
Now it's making me sleepy. I want to go back. *HELP!*

Yelling just didn't turn out right. It sounded like *Ahhhheeeeppp
ahhhheeeeppp*, but then the nurses stared at me with these googly
eyes. I tried screaming *Eeeeuw*, but it just turned out wrong. Is
there something about talking that I haven't learned?

**June 18**
**10:10**AM

I'm tied into some moving object, and I'm facing something
tan. I'm thinking, *Is it some sort of soft wall?* when all of a
sudden I'm interrupted by: "Welcome home, Betsy Bovich!"

**One hour later**

Out of nowhere, all kinds of strange people come. They are
basically playing Hot Potato with me! And when we go into a
building, they scream: "Surprise! Welcome, Elizabeth!" Who
is Elizabeth? My parents have only called me Betsy. I'm lost!
Who am I?

I try to say, "Thank you," but it just comes out wrong again,
and those strangers go all googly-eyed, just like those nurses.

**Later that night**

I can't go to sleep. What if I wake up on Mars? All this
moving around freaks me out. Maybe I'll watch TV. Oooh,
look at this. It's a show about animals. It can't hurt me to
watch this all night. I just hope watching TV doesn't cause
brain sickness.

**Five minutes later**

Hey, look! There's a four-legged yellow thing by the door.
My parents call it Murphy. He's coming toward me. *Eeeeuw!*
He's got a big tongue and it's licking me!

**Thirty minutes later**

# The Story of Me

## Betsy Bovich

JUNE 16, 1997
2:32AM

Oh my. What's happening? I'm moving. Am I dying? I
really don't know!

*AAAHHHHH!* What's that light? I'm dying!

**One Hour Later**

These weird things are looking at me, but now they are . . .
wrapping me up in some kind of soft material. I feel quite
sleepy . . . very sleepy. *Ahhhhhh.*

**June 16**
4:02PM

Now, where am I? I'm in some kind of machine. This is
what it says:

ROTABUCNI

They must have taken me! HELP!*!*! I'm in some kind of
p-p-p-plastic cage! *Get me out of this!* I try yelling to get out

"Astonishing! It's a lie," said Lisa.

"I . . . cannot . . . believe . . . *this!* " Kathy exclaimed while breathing heavily. The three girls were feeling like they were going to *explode!*

But then, Melony thought of something. "Duh!" she scoffed. "Move the coats!" She moved the coats over. She thought Mr. Stritmatter was kidding about the machine he had told the fourth graders about. But he wasn't.

When she split those coats in half, she saw a *mirror!* It was her reflection. "Whoa!" said Melony. "I get it!" And she did get it. YOU can do your homework. YOU can brush your teeth. YOU can do whatever you want.

Now you know that the greatest, most excellent machine is . . . YOU!

# The Stritmatter Machine
## Emily Hollen

O N NOVEMBER 17, 1966, in Windber, Pennsylvania, Melony
was born. Her mom, Mabel, stayed at home while her
dad, Jim, was an electrician. When she grew up . . .
Melony turned nine. She was in fourth grade in Mr.
Stritmatter's class. Every time someone did a great job, he had a
machine that was the greatest ever made, and they were allowed to
see it. It was so excellent and magnificent! It could blow you off
of your feet like you were in a twister. *Literally!*

It had gears, and gizmos, and watts, and all sorts of pieces.
It could brush your teeth, and tie your shoes, and even do your
homework for you! "Wow!" gasped Melony, Kathy, and Lisa.
Kathy and Lisa were her "BFFs."

Once, when Melony was quiet, Mr. Stritmatter said, "Melony,
go ahead! See the machine."

Melony gulped. "Really?" she asked.

"Of course," he said.

*Wow*, Melony murmured in her excited mind. She went to
the school closet. She held out her hand to take hold of the door
handle. Melony touched it. She opened it and saw . . .

She couldn't tell what the machine was. It was just a . . . bunch
of *coats*? "Huh?" Melony asked. "A bunch of coats?" She was
surprised. There wasn't a machine at all!

"So how is the machine?" Kathy and Lisa asked the girl
looking at the machine.

began to cry. Tears came running down my face. I was about to go to my room when I heard a faint *meow*.

I bolted around the house again, now feeling better that Annie was somewhere close and must be alright. I finally came to the last cabinet again and got scared she wouldn't be there. I opened the cabinet, took out the blocks, and there was little Annie.

My heart pounded with joy! Her hair felt soft in my hands. Her left eye winked. I released her from my arms and she pounced . . . pounced with joy! She was just glad we found her, and I was glad we found her too.

# *Meow*

## Alex Maranville

I DON'T KNOW what came over me at the vet that day when the veterinarian opened the door wide carrying a black-and-grey kitten. Her nose was dark, and her paws were wet. She was so scared she was shaking. Perhaps it was how small and harmless she looked, or maybe it was that she just looked darned right cute. I think it was her eyes that captivated me. They twinkled like the stars and danced like the moon. I told my mom it was this cat that I wanted. She stared at the cute kitten for a moment and agreed after a few seconds that the cat was ours!

Oh, was Annie ever trouble, though. She skulked around and hid places, so sometimes we thought she had disappeared altogether. She always turned up, though.

It all happened one Saturday. I was putting together the awesome Lego set I got for Christmas when all of the sudden, there was screeching, and then yelling.

"Annie's gone!"

I jumped, and my sister came running and yelling again: "Alex, Annie's gone!"

My heart pounded hard. I got up *fast* and bolted around the house, tearing things apart. I couldn't imagine life without this little kitten. I checked in every nook of the house, including all of her usual hiding places.

As I pulled open the last cabinet, my eyes began to swell. All there was in front of me was a box of blocks. I sat down and

# Boudy's Accident

## James Innes

LAST YEAR, A few days after my birthday, my mom and I were walking my dog, Zelda. Before we left we told my dad to let the other dog, Boudy, in. While we were walking, we heard whining. We didn't bother, though, because Boudy did that every time we went on a walk. When we came back, we were in for a really big surprise!

When we came back, there were bloody paw prints on the deck. We called Boudy, but he didn't come. We finally found him under the deck, and he was alive. We wrapped his paw with paper towels and taped it with duct tape. After that, my dad put him in the car, and drove him to the animal hospital.

While my dad drove him to the hospital, my brother, Mom, and I cleaned the deck. While we cleaned the deck, my mom found a piece of glass from my brother's science experiment. Boudy probably cut himself on this glass. When my dad came home, everything was alright, and everyone was happy. Boudy limped for a while, until he got better. I was ecstatic because he was alright, and since he is a goofy dog, I love him the most. Now, we make sure not to go out barefoot.

# Old Pops
## Jake Langeman

MY GREAT GRANDPA liked peanut butter with apples. He also played tackle football when he was a kid. He loved NFL football. When his wife went into the hospital and he started growing a beard, people say he just got lazy.

He lived with my grandparents for a couple of years. He always called me by a nickname, something like "Captain." We used to call him "Old Pops" because it was shorter.

He used to play with me and my cousins. We would run up to him and yell, "Come and get me!" We'd run back downstairs and he would stand up and say, "I'm gonna get you!" with his arms stretched out to the sides like a big bear.

We lived with my grandparents for a year and during that time, while we lived in the basement, "Old Pops" lived in my grandparents' room, and my grandparents stayed upstairs.

"Old Pops" died in 2004 the day before Halloween. That's why I don't like Halloween. Now when it is my birthday and it rains people say he is crying.

....

See, that's the thing about real life. It can be as crazy and funny and unpredictable as fiction.

It can also be as moving and heartbreaking and dramatic as fiction.

And that's why we tell stories. Because each story we hear, no matter how irrelevant or small it may seem, has the potential to reveal a little bit more about who we are—about what makes us raise our eyebrows in surprise, what makes us laugh till our stomachs hurt, what makes us weep uncontrollably, what makes us . . . well, for lack of a better word: *us.*

Each one of us has our own, unique story to tell, be it big or small; no two people have the same story, and no two people tell a story the same way. According to the latest census numbers, there are 6,659,909,368 people in the world. That means there are at least 6,659,909,368 unique stories to be told. And counting.

So what are you still reading this introduction for? Put down the book . . . no, wait, read the book cover to cover, *then* put it down. Then go out and start collecting stories. Interview your aunt about the funniest vacation she ever took, corner your kid brother and ask him what super power he'd choose if he could have any super power in the world, write your own story about the last time you were really scared.

And then do it all again, this time with different people and different questions.

Go ahead. Try it. I'll wait.

...

See, that's the thing about real life. It can be as crazy and funny and unpredictable and moving and heartbreaking and dramatic as fiction. Only better, because it's actually true.

*Jennifer Guerra is a cultural arts reporter for Michigan Radio, the NPR affiliate in Ann Arbor. She's also the local host of* Weekend Edition.

# *Introduction*
## Jennifer Guerra

D ID YOU HEAR the one about the squirrel stuck in the attic?
Here, let me set the scene. It's a quiet, cold night in a small suburb somewhere on the east coast. A young couple, just married, is enjoying a relaxing evening by the fireplace in their brand new house . . . when all of a sudden they hear a noise. From upstairs. Lots of noises. Scratching noises. Like something is running around and knocking things over in the attic.

So they call the cops.

And what happens next is pure hilarity. And by hilarity I mean chaos. Cops show up, try to catch squirrel in attic; squirrel bests cops, bolts down attic stairs and hides underneath living room sofa. Cops try to trap squirrel underneath sofa; squirrel bolts out from underneath sofa and runs directly into fireplace, catches tail on fire, and runs directly out of fireplace and back underneath sofa. Sofa catches on fire . . . and well, like I said, chaos ensues.

And that, my friends, is a true story. Tall, but true.

Don't believe me? Then hear it for yourself. One of the cops tells the whole story to *This American Life* radio host Ira Glass. You can go to www.thislife.org and search for "Squirrel Cop."

Go ahead. I'll wait.

to observe their progress. As they accepted our suggestions, we could see the students, patiently, creating something they would later be very proud of. Adjectives jumped off the pages. To enrich this exploration, I encouraged students to incorporate their current reflection on their past experience. Independently, students discovered the challenges they had overcome, the numerous moments of utter joy and excitement, and ultimately, how much they had learned in their lives thus far.

I cannot express how much I enjoyed working with the students of Childs Elementary. Their imaginations, memory, attention to detail, and creative fervor fill up these pages. It is my hope these stories inspire you to take time to remember and record your life experiences. There is nothing more indispensable than what we chose to communicate, the honesty and courage it takes to share, and ultimately the dedication and hard work to get it on paper.

True stories live on, oh yes they do, and this, my fellow reader, is a mighty beautiful thing. Wave your hands in the air, don't be shy, get excited, because there are plenty listening, and reading. All the time. Yes, it is *true*.

— Chrissy Deiger

# *Preface*

"**O**H MY GOSH, you won't believe what happened to me yesterday!" "Guess what?" "I know! That reminds me of last summer when . . . "

Often, we are not aware of the impact of personal storytelling. People, both young and old, are inherently driven to speak of personal experiences. This exercise strengthens our memory, our ability to recall and imagine details, and our capacity to creatively communicate to others. Storytelling bonds us to ourselves, and creates connections with others. Philosophically, it often proves the essence of who we are. Each and every day, our experiences shape our identity, and this is to be shared. Most of all, the process of telling a story is fun. There are no wrong answers, no specific guidelines, Sharing a story gets us excited, sometimes out of our seats. We may speak louder, add sound effects, laugh, and move our hands every which way. During a brainstorming activity with the students of Childs Elementary, this was precisely what happened. With arms waving in the air, often Erin and I had trouble deciding whom to call on next. Their enthusiasm amazed me. Within the first few minutes, I felt the workshop was already a success. The students felt inspired and safe to express themselves. Wonderful! Let's get this on paper!

To my surprise, the room fell silent. Pencils wrote: A Tigers game, a silly visit to the beach, a time of reconciliation with friends. As they wrote, Erin and I met with students individually

# True Stories

| | | |
|---|---|---|
| *Preface* | xi | Chrissy Deiger |
| *Introduction* | 1 | Jennifer Guerra |
| *Old Pops* | 3 | Jake Langeman |
| *Boudy's Accident* | 4 | James Innes |
| *Meow* | 5 | Alex Maranville |
| *The Stritmatter Machine* | 7 | Emily Hollen |
| *The Story of Me* | 9 | Betsy Bovich |
| *Splash-Out!* | 12 | Chathu Jayatissa |
| *Broken Leg* | 14 | Seth Schubert |
| *One-Eye Disaster* | 15 | Hannah Wolf |
| *Pet Store* | 17 | Jake Clark |
| *The Baseball Game* | 19 | Ashley Blackburn |
| *Why Me?* | 21 | Kellie Beck |
| *The Special Cats* | 23 | Sydney Maranville |
| *Sally & the Gigantic Babysitter* | 24 | Taylor Hosein |
| *Part 2: The Fire* | 26 | Alexis McGhee |
| *The Tree* | 27 | Alex Maranville |
| *Partners* | 29 | Autumn Davis |
| *My Water Park Birthday Party* | 30 | Marisa Fitch |

## MANY THANKS TO:

*All the folks at Childs Elementary for letting us
infiltrate their classrooms: Jeff Petzak, Principal;
Patricia Luckscheiter; Kylie Hill; Troy Hansbarger;
Rochelle Sancho; Emily Hicks;
and Rick Schaffner, Curriculum Director.*

*The Childs Parent and Teacher Team (PATT), as well as
the parents who volunteered their time and energy,
specifically: Lori Maranville and Michelle Wolf.*

*826michigan, especially: Erin Bennett, Thaddeus Blotch,
Terry Carpenter, Chrissy Deiger, C. Jason DePasquale,
Anne Ebbers, Mollie Edgar, Chandra Gill,
Jennifer Guerra, Jen Halas, Jared Hawkley,
Ryan Howard, Sean Murphy, Sydney Smith,
Krysta Stone, Amy Sumerton, Amanda Uhle,
and Chris Westoff.*

*Thanks, finally, to Ian Huebert for moving his pen about
a page in such a way that resulted in our beautiful book
cover and interior illustrations.*

Published by BLOTCH BOOKS
*housed within 826michigan*
115 East Liberty Street Ann Arbor MI 48104
www.826michigan.org

Copyright © 826michigan and the authors
June 2008
All rights reserved

ISBN 0-9779289-5-0

All artwork created by Ian Huebert
www.themilkmachine.com
Book design by Amy Sumerton

*true stories*

Involving memoirs, autobiographies, biographies, histories rewritten, & anecdotes of the sort that might make the face go hot & cold because of some undeniable connection to a very dear memory (thereby serving to illustrate a concept which is universally believed true).

**826michigan** is a non-profit organization dedicated to supporting students ages 6 to 18 with their creative and expository writing skills, and to helping teachers inspire their students to write. Our services are structured around our belief that great leaps in learning can happen with one-on-one attention and that strong writing skills are fundamental to future success. Proceeds from the sale of this book benefit free student programming at **826michigan**.

For more information, please visit
**www.826michigan.org.**

# true stories